Delivery Van

WORDS FOR TOWN AND COUNTRY

Betsy and Giulio Maestro

CLARION BOOKS
New York

The full-color art in this book was
prepared in pen and ink with watercolor.
The text type is 18 pt. Melior.

Clarion Books
a Houghton Mifflin Company imprint
215 Park Avenue South, New York, NY 10003
Text copyright © 1990 by Betsy Maestro
Illustrations copyright © 1990 by Giulio Maestro
All rights reserved.
For more information about permission to reproduce
selections from this book, write to Permissions,
Houghton Mifflin Company, 2 Park Street, Boston, MA 02108.
Printed in USA

Library of Congress Cataloging-in-Publication Data
Maestro, Betsy.
    Delivery van : words for town and country / by Betsy Maestro ;
illustrated by Giulio Maestro.
        p.   cm.
    Summary: The reader is introduced to typical town and country
words such as "roadside stand," "village," "dairy farm," and "marina"
as a delivery van and its woman driver travel through a busy
workday.
    ISBN 0-395-51119-4
    1. Vocabulary—Juvenile literature.   2. City and town life—
Juvenile literature.   3. Country life—Juvenile literature.
[1. Vocabulary.   2. City and town life.   3. Country life.]
I. Maestro, Giulio, ill.   II. Title.
PE1449.M323   1990
428.1—dc20
[E]   89-23992
                                                                  CIP
                                                                   AC

WOZ 10 9 8 7 6 5 4 3 2 1

Early in the morning, the delivery van leaves the highway from the city. It is full of packages to be delivered all over the **town** and **countryside.**

The big, blue van turns off **Main Street** and heads into the **shopping center.** Pat, the driver, knows she has many packages to deliver there.

The **hardware store** is the first stop of the day.
Mr. Brown has just opened up. "Morning, Pat," he calls
as she puts his boxes on the counter. They chat for a
minute, and then Pat's on her way.

The van drives by the **bank.** Cars are in line at the
drive-in window. Pat pulls up at her next stop.

There are always lots of packages to bring to the
pharmacy. Today, they are all different shapes and
sizes. When the delivery is finished, Pat calls, "See you
tomorrow," as she heads out the door.

The **parking lot** in front of the **grocery store** is already filling up with cars as the van drives off.

At a **stop sign,** Pat waits until no one is coming.
Then she pulls out toward her next delivery.

The van parks in front of the **town hall.** There is a
package to deliver to one of the offices inside.

Then Pat drives past the **post office** and on up
the street.

At the **library,** the big, blue van stops at the side door. Pat carries in some very heavy boxes. "Oh, great! Our new books are here!" says the librarian. Pat smiles and waves on her way out.

Farther up the street, the van passes the new **movie theater.** It's closed now, but in the evening it will be crowded with people.

As it leaves the town center, the van turns onto a smaller **road.** Pat passes some ducks and a family of swans swimming in a little **pond.**

At the **school,** the van turns in to make a delivery.
Pat carries a few packages into the building. As she
leaves, she waves to the children on the **playground.**
"Hi, Pat!" they call.

Down the road a short way, the van pulls in at the **roadside stand.** It's lunchtime. "Hi, Rosie!" Pat says. "What's good today?"

After eating, Pat stops at the **antique shop.** Mrs. Dudley has a package for her to pick up. It will be delivered to a customer in another town.

At the **country inn,** the delivery van stops again.
Pat carries in a long, white box. "Must be my new
umbrella stand," says Mr. James, the inn's owner.

On the road again, the big, blue van drives farther out
into the country. At a red **mailbox,** it turns down a
long **driveway.**

The **dairy farm** is busy today. The Kellys are expecting some farm tools they've ordered. They're glad to see Pat drive up.

After the delivery, Pat walks over to the **barn** to take
a peek at a new calf, born just yesterday.

On the way out, the van passes a big, green **field** where horses are grazing.

At the bottom of a big **hill,** the van comes into the
village. Pat pulls over to check the remaining packages.

There are three boxes to deliver in the village. Pat carries one to the big, white **house** and another to the **church.**

The **general store** is very quiet when Pat comes in with the third package. Mrs. Appleby is behind the counter. "Hi, Pat," she says. "I just baked some cookies. Have one." "Thanks," says Pat, who is glad to have a little snack.

On the way back toward town, the van makes another stop at the **garden center.** Spring is a busy season, and Pat will be making many deliveries here.

Down the road a bit, the van passes the **marina** along the river. Small boats are bobbing up and down in the water.

There are some tires to be delivered at the **service station.** They're heavy, but Pat rolls them inside. This is the last delivery of the day.

The van comes to a **railroad crossing** and stops.
Pat looks both ways before driving across the tracks.

At the **diner,** Pat stops for a quick cup of coffee before she ends her day. Another driver she knows is at the counter. "Hi, Sam, how was your day?" she asks.

Now it's time for Pat to drive the delivery van back to the city. She heads up the ramp onto the highway. Tomorrow there will be a new load of packages for the van to deliver all over the town and countryside.

About the Author

Betsy Maestro taught kindergarten and first grade for eleven years and earned a master's degree in Elementary Guidance. Since 1974, she has been collaborating with her husband, Giulio, on concept books for young children, including the popular *Harriet* series. They have also created *The Story of the Statue of Liberty* and *A More Perfect Union*, an ALA Notable Book. In 1989, the Maestros began a new group of books for Clarion with *Taxi: A Book of City Words*. *Delivery Van* is their second book in this series.

About the Artist

Giulio Maestro attended the Cooper Union Art School and worked for several years in advertising. He has been illustrating and writing children's books since 1969. Mr. Maestro has illustrated many of Clarion's wordplay books, including five of his own, *Riddle Romp, Razzle-Dazzle Riddles, What's Mite Might?, What's a Frank Frank?,* and *Riddle Roundup.*

The Maestros live in Old Lyme, Connecticut, with their two children, Daniela and Marco.